Trashy The Trashcan

BY - Khwaish Arora   (Book recommended for ages 2-6)

Our world is a place where people are careless about their surroundings. People all over the

world throw little rappers to big pieces of junk thinking that what harm would a little garbage do to the ENTIRE WORLD,

and throw garbage thinking just that. No one realizes that there are infinite people in the world and every single person can make a difference.

But, there was someone that cared for the surroundings and wanted to make a big effort for a big difference. His name was Trashy, Trashy the Trashcan.

Trashy felt sad that his surroundings were getting filthier by the minute and he was even more sad that there was nothing he could do as he was kept in a dark alley where no one usually came. he was also sad because of his size he was so small that he could barely be seen.

One day there was a man walking by. He was eating a banana but when he was done eating, he looked around to see

that if no one was around him and he threw away the banana peel. He didn't feel ashamed at all.

Trashy was behind him and he knew what he had to do.

Trashy called the man and said " What are you doing?". The man was confused and looked around to see who said that. He did not see anyone so he kept on walking. Trashy called the man again and said "Don't you feel ashamed of what you just did. Don't you know where you have to throw your garbage. I was just behind you and I would have been happy if you had thrown your garbage into me and not on the streets.

The man was shocked to see the Trash can talk and then he said " What difference would it make if one banana peel just falls on the street. The world is too big to be completely covered with junk, especially just with my banana peel." The trashcan was surprised to see that some one

really did not care about the environment.
The trashcan replied that " You should really care about the environment, Don't you know how much the environment gives to us. Trees give us many things and do things to make the world a better place for people to live like -

1.Trees clean the air from gases that are very harmful.

2.Trees provide oxygen for us all to breath.

3.Trees give us wood for making houses and furniture.

4.Trees help prevent water pollution.

5.Trees provide food.

6.Trees heal us by giving many medicines.

7.Trees give us bark to make paper.

8.Trees conserve energy.

9.Trees help prevent soil erosion.

And that is just about trees. There are more things in our environment like water, air ,soil, crops, and many minerals too.

And because the food you eat, the clothes you

wear and the home you live in are made from the resources in the environment, So you should care every little piece of junk because it counts for the entire world to be filthy. There are millions and millions of people in the world, and if each person throws garbage, even small garbage, then it won't take much time for the whole world to be covered in trash. And food thrown will be rotten and stinky after sometime. It will spread many diseases and also lead to floods and pollution.

"The man said that " Okay fine, I do realize that I am wrong. But what will happen if only I realize this and no one else, the world will still be a mess." The trash can felt that that was right. He said " There is an easy solution, you just have to

spread the word about keeping the environment clean. There are some easy ways for that to happen like the main rule of Reduce-Reuse-Recycle and also to throw the garbage in trash can like mine or recycling bins of green, blue and many other colors, all used for a different purposes." and "There are many was to keep the environment clean. You just have to keep the spirit and try to do your part in keeping the environment clean.

For starters, you can throw the banana peel on the street into me. "The man felt that he was teaching him the right thing so, he picked up the banana peel he threw on the road and threw it into the trash can. The man thanked Trashy for telling him all the difference he can make in the world.

After he came home he started to make a campaign about keeping the earth clean and to make sure everyone does their part for it. After sometime Trashy saw that streets were getting cleaner and trashcans were getting full.

Trashy was very happy to see that he helped in making a difference. He realized that his size mean anything its just the size of his spirit that helped him. He had no idea that one day he could make such a big difference

The man would not have realized that what he was doing is wrong if Trashy didn't tell him what is right. Because of Trashy a lot of people understood what stuff they should be doing to keep the Earth clean. Now Trashy did his part but now it is time for you do yours.

THE END

Clean and Green Earth